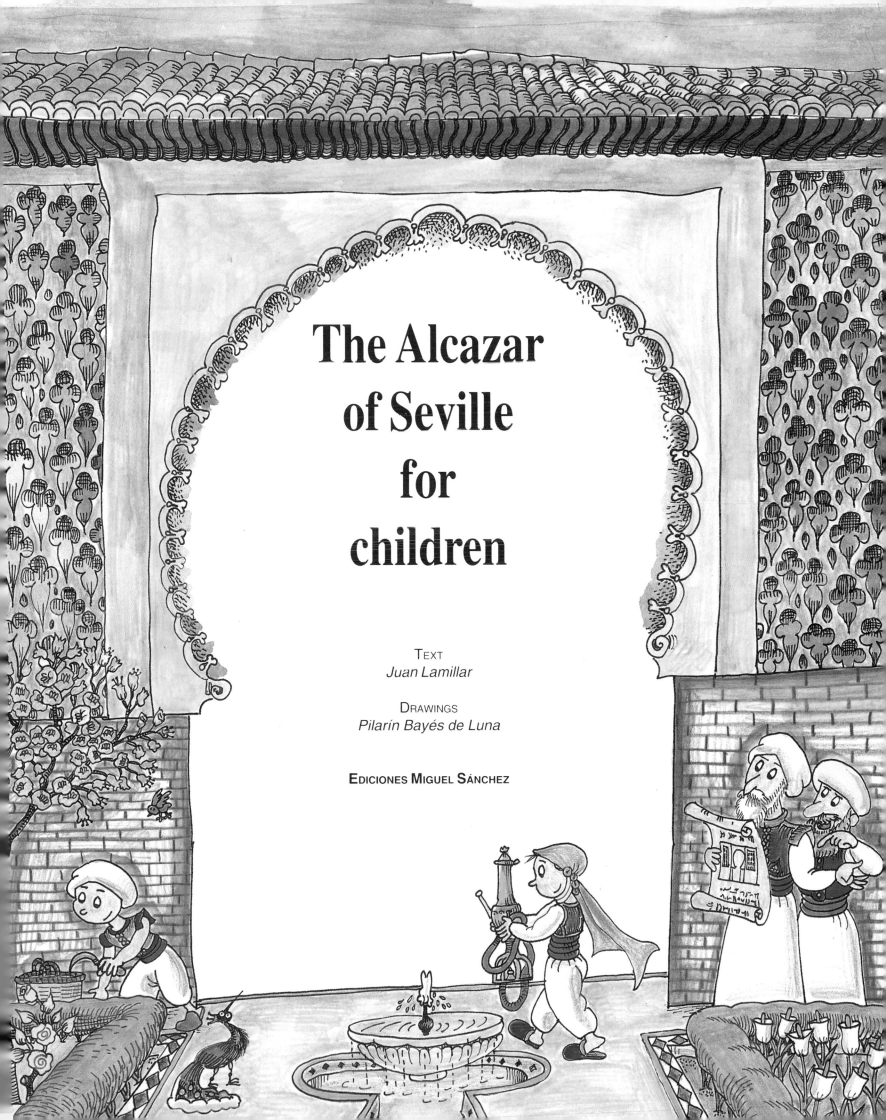

The Alcazar of Seville for children

TEXT
Juan Lamillar

DRAWINGS
Pilarín Bayés de Luna

EDICIONES MIGUEL SÁNCHEZ

© EDICIONES MIGUEL SÁNCHEZ C.B.

c/ MARQUÉS DE MONDÉJAR, 44 – GRANADA

© DRAWINGS : PILARÍN BAYÉS DE LUNA

© TEXT : JUAN LAMILLAR

TRANSLATION : BABEL TRADUCCIONES, S.L. (NICOLA JANE GRAHAM)

PHOTOCOMPOSITION : BITONO (PAQUI ROBLES)

PHOTOMÉCHANICS : PANALITOS S.L.

PRINTING : GRAFIC ЯM COLOR

I.S.B.N.: 84-7169-079-9

LÉGAL DEPOSITORY : GR-1561/2003

The drawings and words of these pages are a guide to understanding History, without being afraid of its solemn capital letter. They are also some small pointers so that you do not get lost in this fantastic labyrinth. Enjoy the complicated itineraries: walking through this place is also a chance to travel in time. You are going to have to use your imagination to go through the different ages and greet the many personalities. Come on and follow me. Let us walk together among walls of stone and vegetation, which were the result of dreams and illusions.

The name of this labyrinth is the Royal Alcazares, but everyone calls it the Alcazar of Seville. Despite this familiarity, we must show it great respect, since it is a distinguished old complex (more than a thousand years old), which has been renovated to give it a youthful appearance. Bear in mind that it is the oldest inhabited Royal Palace in Europe, as it is still used as the residence of the King and Queen of Spain when they visit the city, but at the same time it is a place open to today's cultural life: theatre, concerts and exhibitions.

It was proclaimed a **World Heritage Site** by UNESCO in 1987.

A LOOK AT HISTORY

The city of Seville is almost three thousand years old and it has always liked enhancing its extremely rich history with legends.

The first is about its foundation, no less than by Hercules himself when he came to these Southern lands to avenge the death of his father. Apart from killing Gerion, a king of Tartessos who had three heads, he robbed him of his magnificent red bulls. The Greek hero has not disappeared from Andalusia completely: he forms part of its coat of arms.

Important civilisations have left their mark: the mysterious Tartessians, the Phoenicians, Greeks and Carthaginians. Even Rome touched Seville with a figure that is halfway

between history and myth: Julius Caesar, who came for military reasons and surrounded Hispalis (that was what it was known as then) with some famous ramparts. These defences were renovated in different ages and they were conserved until the end of the 19th century. Some remains can still be seen: the most complete are in the district of La Macarena.

Therefore, Hercules and Julius Caesar have become the symbols of classical Seville.

The Visigoths came after the Romans. We know that they turned the city into a centre of medieval culture, but not many traces of them are left. The Arab invasion took place in 711. The Arabs were in the city for five centuries: Hispalis became known as Isbiliya, the River Betis as Guadalquivir (which means "large river") and different dynasties of rulers succeeded each other: Omeyas, Abassies, Banu Abbad, Almoravides and Almohades. Under the latter's rule the city attained great splendour: we can still see some of their monuments, such as the tower called Giralda (the Muslim part, of course) and the Golden Tower.

The original Alcazar, which was a military complex and a royal palace at the same time, was built at the beginning of the 10th century and successive monarchs extended it. Of all those that lived there, I want you to meet Al-Mutamid, who besides being king was an excellent poet. And as so often happens, poetry formed an alliance with love in the story of his life.

Al-Mutamid was walking along the river bank with his prime minister and he started a poem: "The breeze turns the river / into a coat of mail..." (Remember that a coat of mail was armour made of iron chain mail). A slave woman who was washing finished the poem: "It cannot find a better coat / than the cold freezing it over." The king fell in love with the slave, who was called Itimad, but known as Rumaiquiya, and he made her his wife. The Alcazar was the setting for this love and the queen's whims. As Itimad liked kneading clay, the king filled a pond with camphor, cinnamon and amber and he planted almond trees with extremely white flowers when she wanted to see the snow. Al-Mutamid died in the north of Africa, exiled and a prisoner, missing Seville and the refinements of his court.

But if there is a king whose name is linked with the Alcazar, that is Peter I, for some "the Cruel", for others "the Executor of Justice". Despite being a Christian monarch, when he decided to build his own palace he did it in an Arab style. Between 1364 and 1366, what is today the core of the Alcazar was constructed, and the king, besides the Sevillian master builders, ordered craftsmen to be brought from Granada and Toledo. It is, therefore, a building in the Mudéjar style. (The Mudéjars were the Arabs that lived in Christian territory).

The River Guadalquivir divides the city into two and only a fragile bridge of boats moored with chains joined Seville and the Triana district then (and until the 19th century). Did you know that to conquer the city the ships of King Ferdinand III had to break the chains and destroy the boats, thus isolating the Muslims, who had no other choice but to surrender? That happened in 1248. Seville was once again a Christian city. From then on, the Castilian kings went to live in the Alcazar, but a lot of alterations were made. The first was the Gothic style palace that Alphonse X had built.

ALFONSO X

PEDRO I

Peter I filled this complex and indeed the entire city with legends. The most famous lent its name to a Sevillian street: Cabeza del Rey Don Pedro (which means head of King Peter). On one of his night outings, the king killed a man and he was discovered by an old woman who had recognised the characteristic creaking of the monarch's bones. The king admitted that he was guilty, rewarded the old woman and, as was the custom with murderers, he placed his own head in a corner... but sculpted in stone. If you walk along this central street, you can still see, in a niche, the bust of Peter I with his royal attributes: crown, sceptre and sword.

He wanted to be a just king, and many anecdotes are told about his particular way of understanding justice, but he also ordered the death of people very close to him, such as his wife, Blanche of Bourbon, and his brother. He fell in love with Maria de Padilla: this love affair was much commented on at the time and left its mark on the history of the Alcazar.

The later kings, above all the Catholic Monarchs, continued to alter the building. But the most important work took place in the 16th century.

In this century, Seville was one of the most important cities in the world, as it was the only one that had the privilege of trading with America and it filled up with foreign merchants, and there was a great deal of trade in gold and silver.

And a very important fact: emperor Charles V decided to marry Isabella of Portugal in Seville. The Alcazar was the setting for the wedding, which took place in March 1526. There were great celebrations in the city, which had all become an improvised theatre: triumphant arches were erected in the streets, jousts and tournaments were held, ambassadors came from many countries, as well as poets, such as Juan Boscán and Garcilaso de la Vega.

The Alcazar continued to have strong links with the Spanish crown. There were kings that hardly visited it and others, such as Philip V, in the 18th century, who lived in the Alcazar from 1729 to 1733 and transferred the court to Seville. The last great works of the Alcazar were carried out after the Lisbon earthquake in 1755, which damaged the building. Since then, it has often been restored.

In the sixties of the 18th century, the erudite of Seville (those who believed in progress and wanted social reform) met in the Alcazar at the famous gatherings of Pablo de Olavide, who was a governor who started to modernise the city. He greatly admired a French philosopher, Voltaire, and he had many problems with the Church of that age. Olavide ordered the first "scientific" map of Seville to be made.

At the beginning of the 19th century, after the French invasion, the new king of Spain was Joseph Bonaparte, Napoleon's brother. When he stayed in Seville he chose the Alcazar as his residence. Although the French were not in the city for very long, they carried out urban improvements, but when they left, after being defeated in the War of Independence, they took many important paintings with them from Sevillian churches.

And, among so many kings, there was a queen in the 19th century: Isabella II, who spent a great deal of time at the Alcazar and had important alterations done.

Alphonse XIII often visited this palace and resided in it during his reign in the first decades of the 20th century as a result of the Ibero-American Exposition which was held in Seville in 1929. So that you can get an idea of what it was like, it was an Expo like those we have nowadays (Seville in 1992, Lisbon in 1998) and many of the buildings constructed then have become monuments: for example, the Plaza de España or the pavilions of the Plaza de América in the Maria Luisa park.

The official residence of the king and queen of Spain is currently in the part called the top Royal Quarter, which has recently been opened up to the public again after many years of not being able to visit it. We can now look at the small and marvellous oratory of Isabella the Catholic, with its tiled altar. But most striking in these twenty-two rooms (halls, offices, bedrooms, dining room…) is the contrast between the Mudéjar decoration of the walls with tiles and plasterwork, the old coffered ceilings, and the furniture, lamps and paintings

of the 19th century, almost all from when Isabella II lived in the Alcazar.

The last great event held at the Alcazar was the wedding reception of Princess Elena of Bourbon in March 1995. As in the glorious days of old, the city welcomed members of the Royal Houses and of European nobility and turned the ceremony into a real party for the people.

A STROLL THROUGH THE ALCAZAR

The word **alcazar,** of Arabic origin, has the double meaning of fortress and royal palace, and the two coincide in this complex of buildings. Here it is, surrounded by strong high ramparts. But, before you reach it, you will no doubt have passed through some cheerful squares which contain the most famous monuments in the city. You will have seen the imposing cathedral, one of the greatest in Christianity, with its tower, which is the symbol of Seville: the Giralda. At first it was the minaret of the mosque and in the 16th century Hernán Ruiz added an elegant bell tower to it, he harmonised the Muslim and the Christian aspects beautifully and he crowned it with a large bronze weather vane, known as the Giraldillo.

In such a short walk, you will have seen examples of different artistic styles: the gothic Cathedral, the baroque Archbishop's palace and the renaissance Archive of the Indies, which was formerly the Exchange building (the place where the merchants did their business) and now holds the most complete documentation on Spanish America.

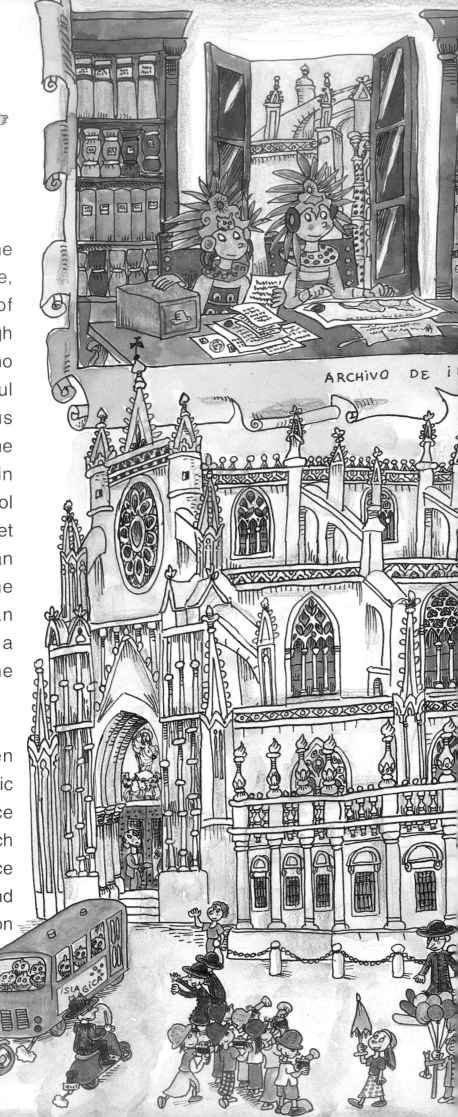

ARCHIVO DE I

VIRGILIO

1691

Your first stop is the **Hall of Justice,** built by Alphonse XI, closely imitating the decoration of some halls of the Alhambra. According to legend, the murder of Master Fadrique took place here, ordered by his brother, King Peter. Next to this hall is the **Plaster Courtyard,** a jewel of Almohade architecture, and the oldest part of the Alcazar you are going to see: delicate and elegant, with a beautiful series of arches and a central pool, it was built in the 12th century.

Going through one of the gates which open up in the long stretch of ramparts, we arrive at the

But now you are in front of the ramparts. The Alcazar is entered through the **Lion Gate.** There is a medieval lion on it, painted on some tiles, inviting us to visit it with its motto "Be prepared for everything", which is a quote from *The Aeneid,* the famous Latin poem by Virgil. We do as it says and we are now in the **Lion Courtyard.** In the 17th century there was a theatre here, the largest in the city, known as the Corral de la Montería (Hunting Yard). As these shows were the main entertainment of the time, it was often used until a fire destroyed it in 1691.

DON FADRIQUE

Hunting Courtyard. Its name conjures up the kings' love of hunting. This courtyard was where the nobles gathered, armed and ready to accompany the king on his days out hunting. Imagine the horses and falcons, bows and scimitars, the colourful costumes and standards.

From this courtyard you are going to enter one of the halls that form part of the House of Trade of the Indies, founded by the Catholic Monarchs to control commerce with the recently discovered America. In these chambers Queen Isabella received Christopher Columbus after his second voyage. Only two parts are still standing today: the **Admiral's Hall,** with its beautiful ceiling dating from the 16th century and adorned with spectacular paintings from the 19th and 20th centuries, which is usually used for official events, and the **Audience Hall,** whose beautiful giltwood ceiling, tapestried walls, coats of arms of famous admirals and, above all, **altar retablo of the Virgin of Seafarers or Navigators** are all bound to surprise you. Painted by Alejo Fernández in the 16th century, the retablo is the first existing representation of the discovery of America. Under the Virgin's protective mantle, you can see the portraits of Christopher Columbus, Charles V, Américo Vespuccio... If you look carefully at the lower part of the painting, you will see some examples of the ships of the time.

Palace of Peter I.– Peter I led the life of a sultan rather than that of a Christian king in Seville. The facade of his palace is wonderful, isn't it? For some it is like a large tapestry in which brickwork, the grace of the arches and the colour of the ceramics are harmoniously interwoven. By the way, that large blue band under the majestic carved wooden eaves crowning the facade repeats the motto of the Nasrid emirs in Arabic writing again and again: "Only God wins". Another inscription in Spanish states that it was the "powerful" and "conquering" Peter I who had the palace built.

The palace is entered through a somewhat mysterious hallway with two corridors. One takes us to the part where the king's public life took place and the other to his private rooms. If we go down the first one, we end up in the **Courtyard of the Maidens.** The first impression is of space and elegance. I am sure you love this harmony of arches and columns and the colourful tiles. Take note of the doors, the marvellous work of carpenters from Toledo. Concerts are usually held in this courtyard: imagine the magic of music added to the marvels of the architecture.

Peter I only prepared two rooms in the top part, the office and the bedroom. You will realise that the upper gallery is different, as it is renaissance style, and it was built in the 16th century. The original columns of the courtyard were also changed for the ones you can see now, which were brought over from the most famous Italian workshops.

You will enter the **bedroom of the Moorish Monarchs,** which were the King's summer rooms, the **Prince's Room,** which is called that because Prince John, the son of the Catholic Monarchs, was born there (do not forget to look up: the coffered ceilings are lovely), the **Catholic Monarchs' ceiling room,** which has a frieze in which "Tanto monta" ("It makes no difference") is repeated, which was the Monarchs' motto.

The best thing to do here is to walk around slowly paying a great deal of attention to the different connected rooms, each one with their own decoration and anecdotes. I am sure that after having visited the Courtyard of the Maidens, you will be surprised by the **Courtyard of the Dolls,** which is almost a miniature. It got its name from some small heads that can be seen on the springing of one of the arches. The courtyard is extremely beautiful, with delicate craftwork, but I have to tell you that only the ground floor is original. The mezzanine and the top gallery were added in the 19th century, copying the plasterwork of the Alhambra.

As the coffered ceilings are so varied and so important artistically, they often lend their name to the different rooms. So you will have to go on looking up in **Philip II's ceiling hall,** which is an elongated room with a striking renaissance coffered ceiling, which means that it is also known as the **Hall of Coving.** The **Arch of the Peacocks** opens up in one of its end walls, with three very adorned arches, with small lattice windows, typically Arab, and with representations of peacocks and other birds. Through this very solemn arch we arrive at the most important and spectacular room of the Mudéjar palace: the **Hall of the Ambassadors or of the Throne.**

All the richness and the beauty of the previous rooms are multiplied in this sumptuous hall, with a truly splendid semispherical cupola made of giltwood: its ribbon work traces stars. As a result of its shape, it was formerly known as the **Half Orange Hall.**

This was the original throne room of the Muslim Palace and Peter I reused it, adorning it with a tiled skirting and covering its walls with very richly adorned and colourful arabesques. The cupola you are admiring was built in 1427. At the end of the 16th century four turned iron balconies were added, supported by winged dragons, which connect with the rooms of the upper Royal Quarter. They are also magnificent works of light ironwork.

Keep looking up: cupola, balconies and now a frieze which runs around the entire perimeter of the hall and which is a gallery of the Spanish monarchs, from the Goth Rescesvinto to Philip III. To complete the boxes the portraits of thirty-two ladies appear. And there is still more: I wonder if you can find the four animals: dog, cat, dove and falcon.

This hall has a legend of death: here Peter I killed the king of Granada Mohamed VI, known

as the "Red king" as he was a redhead. But it also has a love story: Charles V and Isabella of Portugal married under this cupola.

Still dazzled by such splendour, we have to continue through other rooms, such as the **Hall of Princes or Charles V's ceiling room**, which was the palace's old chapel. The renaissance ceiling is made of dark cedar wood, extremely well carved, and we can see the Emperor's symbols on the wooden frieze supporting it: the two-headed eagle and the columns with the motto: "Plus Ultra".

Gothic Palace.– Returning to the Hunting Courtyard, an 18th century corridor takes us to

was interested in poetry (he wrote the *Cantigas de Santa Maria)* and history. He had books of oriental tales translated and others that were about games, such as chess, or about sciences, such as astronomy. He loved Seville a great deal, a city that was loyal to him when he had to confront his son Sancho. That is why he granted various tiles to Seville and he added a motto to his coat of arms: "Seville has not abandoned me". He is buried in the Royal Chapel of the Cathedral, as are Peter I and Saint Ferdinand.

the **Courtyard of the Crossing or of Maria de Padilla,** which was originally an Almohade palace (12ᵗʰ century) constructed on two levels. If you cross it, you will come to the old Gothic palace that Alphonse X the Wise had built and which was then modified in the times of Charles V. In the Middle Ages it was known as the **Spiral Room** because it has this type of staircase in its towers, today it has the name of **Charles V's Rooms.**

The court of Alphonse X, who was a king very concerned with culture, gathered in them. He

VICTOREM CAROLUS TER GRATA
SALUTANT, HASAMUM CÆSAR QUAH
VIS NIL POLLICITUM CUM RE NEC

In the **Hall of Tapestries** you can see some very valuable tapestries that tell us about the conquest of Tunisia (in the north of Africa), one of Charles V's most famous military exploits. Do not forget to take a look at the chapel, which is very simple, and in which the retablo of the Antigua Virgin stands out. Only very recently has it been possible to admire a youthful work by Velazquez there: *Saint Ildefonso being conferred the chasuble,* his best painting in the city.

Years later, these rooms were the residence of Maria de Padilla. They still conserve the strong Gothic vaults, although the atmosphere reminds us of the Renaissance. This is where the Emperor's wedding reception was held, so they are also known as the **Celebration Rooms.** At the end of the 16th century the walls were lined with extremely beautiful tiles that paid tribute to the Emperor and presented him as a hero.

From these rooms we go into that other labyrinth I told you about at the beginning, not now of walls, but of vegetation: **the gardens.**

The Gardens.- One of the most appealing features about the Alcazar is its gardens, so loved by the Arabs. From their origins, stones and plants were linked in this complex, and grew together. Nowadays, the gardens cover an extensive surface area (seven hectares), in which you will see different types of garden, from those that are closer to the original ones to those that were planted last century.

I will repeat here the advice I gave to you for the building: take a stroll and let your imagination wander as well: everything you are going to see is beautiful; on the other hand, pay attention to the small details and try to guess where one garden ends and the next begins. I am sure you will get it right because the limits are very clear. And it will be all the better if you like botany, because you will see many species here, all living in harmony, with the abundance of tall palm trees as the dominant feature.

The old Muslim orchards that surrounded the palaces were transformed over time and in the 16th century the ambassador of Venice, Andrea Navagero, described these gardens as "a forest of orange trees where the sun does not penetrate and it is perhaps the most peaceful place there is in all of Spain".

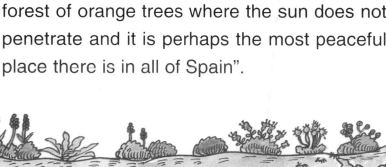

When you go down from Charles V's rooms, the first thing you will see is **Mercury's Pond,** which symbolises trade. The fountain with the sculpture of the god, all made of bronze, was cast by Bartolomé Morel, whose workshops were also responsible for the Giradillo. Next to this fountain, Garcia Lorca read out the *Lament for the Death of a Bullfighter,* which is one of the best poems in Spanish Literature, to a group of Sevillian friends in 1935. Poetry has always had a privileged place in the Alcazar (remember the authors we have mentioned: Al-Mutamid, Boscán, Garcilaso) and soon you will go through a garden, designed in the fifties last century, which is called the Garden of the Poets.

The **Grutescos Gallery** starts behind the pond, separating the old gardens from the more modern ones. The grutescos, which try to reproduce the roughness of real caves artificially, were used here to hide the old Arab ramparts and they were constructed of volcanic rock. A good thing to do is to go up to the gallery and to walk along it as if you were sentries. You will have the best view of the gardens from the top.

And from the heights to the underground. Crossing in front of the pond again, we will arrive at the **Garden of the Dances,** which was named thus because there were some mythological figures here in the 16th century, which seemed to be dancing. On the right-hand side of this garden is the entrance to the **baths of Maria de Padilla,** which is the underground part of the Crossing Garden that I mentioned to you a while back. I am sure you will find this singular place mysterious: the gothic vaults, the large pool where it is known that Maria Padilla bathed, and at the back there is a cave fountain that was added in the 16th century.

Whether you are paying attention or have your head in the clouds, your steps will take you from one garden to another. You should be aware of the names: **Ladies, Cross, Galley, Prince, Troy,** each one with its special charm, with the same invitation to rest or to let your imagination run away with you. We will soon arrive at the garden of the **Arbour of the Bed Chamber.** Here you will be able to go to a beautiful pavilion that will no doubt have already captured your attention when you saw it from the grutescos gallery. And rightly so, because it is extremely beautiful, surrounded by galleries with Italian columns, walls lined with Triana ceramics, which even then were highly valued, very original flooring and it even has a fountain inside. As a result of its location in the centre of the gardens, it is an ideal retreat to spend the heat of siesta time in the summer. It is known as the **Pavilion of Charles V** and it was built in the first half of the 16th century.

Close by is the **Lion Pavilion,** which got its name from the lion that looks over the pond. And the **labyrinth** is also nearby, made of myrtle, where you will no doubt want to get lost. But do not worry. It is not very difficult to find the way out.

Retracing our steps a little and crossing the wall through the **Gate of Privilege,** we enter the new gardens, which are of last century. As you are by now experts at differentiating styles, perhaps you will be surprised by a gate that seems to be a little out of place.

Indeed this monumental gate, of late gothic style, the **Marchena Gate,** was not constructed here, since it comes from a palace in the city of Seville also called Marchena. King Alphonse XIII bought it at the beginning of last century at an auction and it was transferred to these gardens.

Going through it, we start to get near the exit. You will still have the chance to see other gardens and courtyards on the way to the **Carriage Yard,** which is the Alcazar's other exit. You will no doubt notice the set of columns which give this area an air of elegance, which the carriages of previous centuries adorning the passageway enhance. Through a

But before you venture into the streets of this district —another labyrinth you should not mind getting lost in- you must look in front of you from the very gateway of the Alcazar with attention and excitement: there are quite a few centuries that you have experienced in a few hours. On the battlements of the ramparts, the very tower that accompanied us to the Lion

magnificent facade of the start of the 17th century, we go into the **Courtyard of Flags,** which was the weapons courtyard of the original Arab Alcazar. In the same side of the facade an arch opens up which will lead you to the Santa Cruz district, which formed part of the old Jewish quarter. Along the street called **Callejón del Agua,** which means water alley, you can walk protected by more of the Alcazar's ramparts, which were recently restored. The pipes that supplied the palace with water ran through them.

Gate now bids farewell and seems to ask you if you had a good time inside there, which ghosts you made friends with and if you are thinking of coming back soon. These are the questions with which the Giralda says goodbye to curious children who are not afraid of History with a capital H.

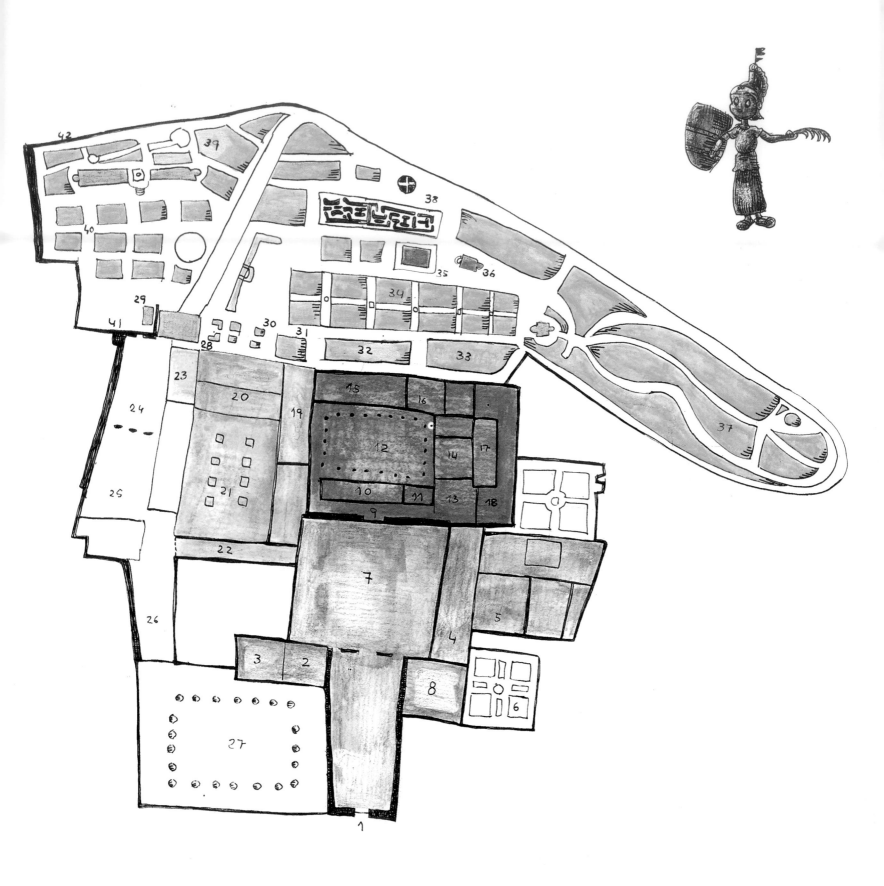

OLD ALCAZAR

PALACE OF PETER I

GOTHIC PALACE

GARDENS